Discover and Unleash the Nous of
Leadership by

LEADING
WITH
REFINED MINDSET

Be the brave and better leader that you
desire.

By
Raymond A. Mills

TABLE OF CONTENT

Introduction:

Bravery, the key quality of a leader.

People have been looking for the exact combination of things that makes up effective leadership throughout history. Great leaders are considered to exhibit strong but prudent judgment, brave but calculated risk-taking, and an assertive but introspective mindset in measured proportions. The wants and demands of the people being led complicate the situation. Leaders who are decisive but inclusive, who have the capacity for both emotional and cognitive intelligence, and who exhibit humility and confidence are those whom followers desire to follow.

Bravery or Courage is a leadership quality that informs and strengthens all the others, or, more correctly, it is a virtue.

Being brave involves being audacious, self-assured, and wise. Being brave does not mean acting carelessly; it requires thought, consideration, and a solid foundation. I have witnessed a lot of folks who, while feigning bravery, were actually being reckless. Having the moral fortitude to act bravely is important. The courageous have a place in leadership. The skill and willingness of leaders to be daring are crucial for teams to function effectively in today's world of ever increasing change.

If organizations are to thrive, they need more leaders who are committed to cultivating a culture of bravery. If business leaders want to succeed, they need to be willing to make brave choices for their employees and communities. And if leaders want to strengthen their organizations and make their teams more effective, they need to develop brave relationships with people who disagree with them.

Leadership and daring, together with employee wellbeing, mental health, and productivity, are "connected like a chain made of the strongest steel.

Courage, according to Aristotle, is the prerequisite for all other virtues, making it the first virtue. It is not only the most significant attribute of a human being but also the most significant attribute of a business. As you consider: Without bravery, other crucial business principles such as sales, innovation, and leadership wither. Making risky, frequently unpopular judgments is a must for leadership. It takes guts to lead.

All of us, to varying degrees, possess these characteristics. When we don't feel brave, courage still exists within us. Each and every person has the capacity to "courage" a terrifying next move, their integrity, or their future. Self-improvement and constructive transformation result from acting courageously. To summon courage at any time, ask yourself, "How can I summon courage in this moment?"

To work on your "courage muscle," dedicate the next month to being courageous. Every day, schedule time and plan for courageous acts big or small in your calendar. Each courageous act feeds the next. Take notice. Watch how confident and empowered you'll feel and how much more you'll accomplish when you're not held back by fear.

A daring leader must possess strength, originality, intelligence, and the ability to accept ambiguity. It entails keeping a positive outlook, being prepared to take calculated risks for the greater good, adapting to constantly shifting circumstances, and remaining genuinely interested about your team and what they can achieve.

In terms of leadership, courage is the ultimate tool that enables you to overcome any obstacle in your path and escape the enemy (FEAR) unscathed.

The followers look to you as a leader to display courage so that they may rely on you or your judgment without reservation.
You may inspire drive in your team, build trust among them, and set a good example by being courageous.

Most significantly, courage is a quality that enables a leader to act on instinct, take risks, and propose novel concepts or solutions.

To put it briefly, good leadership is characterized by courage.

Chapter 1. Leadership in view

Taking chances and questioning the status quo are key components of leadership. Leaders inspire followers to take new and improved actions. It's interesting to note that leaders pursue innovation, not because it's required of them. By examining the accomplishments and knowledge gained by the team, they gauge success. Leaders aren't necessarily those with higher positions within an organization. However, they are individuals who are respected for their morals and work habits. A leader is enthusiastic about their work and shares that excitement with their team members, helping them to accomplish their objectives. Here are what makes up strong leadership.

HONESTY AND INTEGRITY: Leaders place a high importance on virtue and integrity. They are supported by folks who share their convictions.

INSPIRATION: Because they are self-driven, leaders are excellent influencers. They offer their fans some solid motivation. They assist others in comprehending their jobs within a wider framework.

EFFECTIVE COMMUNICATION ABILITIES: Leaders are excellent communicators. With their team, they are open and honest, sharing both their accomplishments and disappointments.

VISION: Visionaries are those who lead: They are quite clear about their goals and how to get there. Leaders can successfully communicate their vision to the team by being effective communicators.

LEADERS ATTACK THE EXISTING QUO WITH A NEVER-GIVE-UP ATTITUDE: They therefore don't easily give up. They also have unique ways to solve a problem.

INTUITIVE: According to leadership consultant Hortense le Gentil, leaders should rely on their intuition when making difficult choices. Particularly because intuition largely draws on one's prior knowledge and life experiences, which makes it more beneficial in challenging circumstances.

EMPATHY: A leader should possess emotional intelligence and empathy because these qualities will enable them to forge close bonds with their team. These characteristics will also aid a leader in responding to the issues, grievances, and goals of his team.

OBJECTIVE: Although empathy is a crucial trait a leader must possess, it is not advisable to let emotions get in the way of making crucial business decisions. Consequently, a good leader should be Objective

INTELLIGENCE: **A successful leader must possess** the intellect necessary to find pragmatic answers to complex issues. A leader should also be analytical and consider the advantages and disadvantages before taking a stand. With the help of an all-encompassing leadership development program, this trait can be honed.

CREATIVITY AND OPEN-MINDEDNESS: **A successful leader is** someone who is receptive to fresh concepts, options, and viewpoints. Understanding that there is no one correct method to do something makes you an excellent leader. A successful leader is therefore constantly prepared to listen, observe, and be open to change. They encourage their teams to think creatively and unconventionally as well. All of these topics will be covered in the curriculum if you sign up for a leadership course.

PATIENCE: A smart leader is aware that it takes time for a business strategy to materialize and provide benefits. They also think that success comes from "continuous improvement and patience."

ADAPTABLE: Since leaders are familiar with the idea of "continuous improvement," they are also aware that this quality will help them succeed. Nothing goes according to plan. Therefore, being adaptable and intuitive aids a manager in maintaining control in challenging circumstances.

What a Leader Does
The following are a leader's primary responsibilities in an organization:

NECESSARY AT ALL LEVELS
Leadership is a role that is significant at all management levels. Obtaining cooperation

at the highest level is crucial for the creation of plans and policies. It is necessary for the interpretation and execution of plans and programs created by the top management at the medium and lower level. When plans are being carried out, leadership can be demonstrated by advising and guiding the subordinates.

REPRESENTATION OF THE ORGANIZATION

A manager, or leader, is referred to as the enterprise's representation.

At forums, conventions, general meetings, etc., he or she must speak on behalf of the issue. His or her responsibility is to explain the business's justification to the public at large. He/she also serves as a spokesperson for the division he/she directs.

RECONCILES AND INTEGRATES PERSONAL GOALS WITH ORGANIZATIONAL GOAL

A leader's leadership qualities assist in bringing together or integrating employees' individual goals with those of the company.

A leader strives to coordinate people's efforts toward a shared goal in order to accomplish goals. This is only possible if he has the ability to persuade people to cooperate willingly and feel the need to achieve the goals.

Seeks Support

In addition to being a manager, a leader also entertains and invites the support and cooperation of subordinates. His personality, intelligence, maturity, and experience can all help him achieve success in this.

In this sense, a leader must solicit suggestions and, if practical, incorporate them into business goals and programs. In this approach, he can get the workers' full cooperation, which increases their willingness to work and, ultimately, a company's effectiveness.

A LEADER MUST POSSESS THREE-DIMENSIONAL QUALITIES THAT MAKE HIM A FRIEND, PHILOSOPHER, AND MENTOR

He can be a friend by discussing his thoughts, feelings, and aspirations with the staff. By employing his knowledge and expertise, a leader can be a philosopher, directing the team as and when the situation calls for it. He or she can act as a mentor by overseeing personnel, explaining top management plans and policies to them, and securing their cooperation to accomplish a concern's objectives. Through problem-solving techniques and counseling, he can occasionally even assume the position of a counselor. He is able to hear the issues that the staff is having and work to find solutions.

The Value of Leadership

Management's crucial role in leadership contributes to efficiency optimization and the accomplishment of organizational objectives. The value of leadership in a situation is supported by the following arguments:

Initiates Action: A leader starts the work by transmitting the policies and plans to the subordinates, from where the work truly begins. A leader is a person who starts the work.

Motivation: A leader demonstrates that they are playing a motivating role in the operation of the company. He inspires the workers with monetary and non-monetary benefits and procures work from the subordinates as a result.

Giving instructions: A leader must not only supervise their subordinates but also act as a source of direction for them. Giving instructions to subordinates on how to carry out their tasks successfully and efficiently is referred to as guidance in this context.

Creating Confidence: Building confidence is crucial, and it can be done by communicating your work efforts to your team members, making sure they understand their roles, and providing them with instructions on how to reach their objectives. It's also crucial to listen to the employees' concerns and grievances.

Fostering Morale: Building morale entails encouraging people to cooperate willingly with their work, gaining their confidence, and earning their trust. By securing complete cooperation, a leader may increase morale and enable employees to work to the best of their ability toward attaining their objectives.

Creates a productive environment: Management relies on its employees to complete tasks. A productive workplace promotes sound and steady growth. Consequently, a leader should keep human interactions in mind. He ought to interact with them on a personal level, listen to their issues, and find solutions. He ought to show compassion to his workers.

Coordination: By balancing individual interests with organizational objectives, coordination can be achieved. The main goal of a leader should be to properly and effectively coordinate in order to achieve this synchronization.

Management and Inspiration

A person can accomplish their goals with the aid of motivation, a feature that is goal-oriented. It encourages someone to put in a lot of effort to accomplish their goals. To affect motivation, an executive needs to possess the appropriate leadership qualities. However, motivation does not have a set design.

One should maintain an open mind about human nature as a leader. Making decisions will undoubtedly be simpler if you are aware of the various needs of your employees.

Both an employee and management need to be capable of inspiring others. A solid understanding of what motivates people is essential for a good leader. He or she must be aware of the fundamental requirements of peers, subordinates, and superiors. Other people are motivated by leadership.

The following are crucial recommendations that explain the fundamental perspective of motivation:

ALIGN THE SUBORDINATE'S NEEDS WITH THE REQUIREMENTS OF THE ORGANIZATION.

The executive has a responsibility as a manager to make sure that the company upholds the same values and principles that he expects of his staff. He or she should see to it that the subordinates are supported and instructed in a way that satisfies the requirements of the company.

THE KEY FACTORS INFLUENCING SOMEONE TO ACCOMPLISH A GOAL ARE APPRECIATION AND REWARDS.

Giving a modest gesture of appreciation, a certificate, or a note in recognition of exemplary or exceptional behavior can be a fantastic motivator. If a certificate is given to a person, it should specify the specific behavior or trait for which the person is being honored.

SETTING AN EXAMPLE FOR OTHERS TO FOLLOW CAN BE A POWERFUL MOTIVATOR FOR OTHERS TO ACHIEVE THEIR GOALS.

For his followers to develop and successfully complete their objectives, a leader must lead by example. •Involving people in planning and major issue resolution processes not only inspires them but also teaches them about the nuances of these crucial decision-making variables. Additionally, everyone will benefit from having a better grasp of their position within the firm. The communication will be clear and unequivocal, and the leader will undoubtedly acknowledge and appreciate it.

Building moral character and a sense of teamwork is undoubtedly important for an organization's success. A person's moral fabric is made up of their mental or emotional state. The decisions and actions of a leader have an impact on his followers' morale. He should therefore be conscious of his choices and actions at all times. The essence of business is teamwork. The leader should always ensure that his team members like working together to complete tasks and participate in the organization's plans

A LEADER SHOULD PUT THEMSELVES IN THEIR FOLLOWERS' POSITIONS AND SEE THINGS FROM THEIR PERSPECTIVE.

He/she ought to sympathize with them in trying circumstances. Their mental and emotional toughness increases when others can relate to their personal struggles.

Achieving a difficult and fulfilling task fosters a sense of accomplishment among workers. The executive must convey to their team members that their labor is crucial to the success and well-being of the company. They are motivated to achieve their goals by this component. Keep in mind that you must be self-motivated if you want to be an effective leader. You must be aware of who you are, what you need, and how strongly you are driven to act in order to attain your objectives.

Only when you have self-motivated yourself can you inspire others to accomplish their own goals and align them with the organization's common objectives.

Leading with Emotional Intelligence Individuals make up an organization, and when individuals are engaged, emotions invariably come into play. This is also true in the workplace. It wouldn't be good to suppose that a workplace is all objective, no-emotion-only performance, like a tightly crowded chamber where hormones have no chance to come in, but the reality is that emotions alone are the strongest motivator or de-motivator of an employee.

If this were not the case, we would never have discussed the value of work-life balance or the requirement for emotionally savvy leaders in the current setting. Emotions alone regulate the performance and efficiency of a worker.

The current period is tremendously dynamic, both economically and socially, with the social fabric changing quickly as a result of globalization and other factors. The workforce is getting younger on average, and leaders are more eager to manage employees from all backgrounds and cultures. It is crucial for a leader in such a circumstance to be particularly sensitive to the emotional components of his or her interactions with individuals.

Emotional intelligence fundamentally refers to the capacity to acknowledge, comprehend,

and use one's own and others' feelings and emotions in order to manage relationships and emotions. Daniel Goleman identified the following four crucial elements of EI:
Self Awareness
Self Management
Social Awareness
Relationship Management or Social Skills

The People's motivation and thoughts are frequently greatly influenced by a leader.
He or she can inspire followers with optimism and confidence and direct them toward positive endeavors, which is known as resonance. On the other hand, they can negatively influence followers and drive them toward destruction, for example, with leaders like Hitler and Osama Bin Laden, which is known as dissonance, the opposite of resonance.

Leaders' body language, facial expressions, and other behaviors are constantly scrutinized.

It is crucial for a leader to take nonverbal cues into account because they can have a favorable or negative impact on followers. As a result, when a leader discusses business ethics while wearing a slightly doubtful and perplexed expression, the followers take note, but the message is not understood by them. A leader must also serve as an example by putting his beliefs, ideals, and principles into practice.

It is challenging to follow the advice of a leader who is not self-aware; one must be aware of one's own strengths and flaws in order to be a good leader. Leaders must have empathy for their subordinates' circumstances, feelings, aspirations, and motives in order to effectively manage them.

A team member's performance may be declining for a variety of reasons. For example, a disruptive employee may be struggling with motivation, while a subordinate who verbally abuses others may be lacking confidence in his own skills. A leader must be able to distinguish between facts, reach deeper levels, and comprehend issues that are not immediately apparent.

Emotional intelligence is crucial for the reasons listed above and also because followers and subordinates expect it from their leaders. Working closely with the management, a subordinate would anticipate that the boss would be aware of his priorities and position. Not unexpectedly, the manager's decision to do so will influence the employee's level of dedication and productivity at work. A leader must appropriately recognize and comprehend when to give orders and when to delegate. He or she must be aware of the moments when the team acts as a single entity and those moments when there are variances.

Although it might be difficult at times, leaders must recognize the necessity and relevance of dealing with the emotional components of interpersonal interactions since they have a significant impact on performance outcomes.

Feedback must be given in an appropriate manner when conducting reviews and growth discussions. The leader must be attentive to the worries and anxieties of the followers, which may occasionally be revealed and occasionally remain hidden. It is much more crucial at the top level because senior executives find it difficult to articulate their concerns and differences, and the leader must prepare for some of them.

Therefore, a leader needs to brush up on his people skills and emotional intelligence because not all of them are born with the charm to hold people in order to be able to attract and retain brilliant subordinates and keep them motivated. Fortunately, emotional intelligence can be improved with repetition and thoughtful effort.

Chapter 2. Managing Vulnerability

The idea of being vulnerable has become popular in recent years. We are advised to make advantage of this "gift of vulnerability" to foster relationships based on mutual respect and kinship.

However, you should be extremely cautious about being "vulnerable" if you want to establish and scale a substantial organization, be an effective manager, or leader. It may put you in danger and leave you vulnerable to abuse.

Being overly familiar with individuals can be a sign that you are "vulnerable," and there is a chance that this could be used against you.

This risk exists whether you're starting your own firm or attempting to move up the corporate ladder. Your authority and standing as a leader could unintentionally be compromised and eroded in either situation by individuals who are eager to take advantage of your weaknesses. Had you not disclosed them so blatantly, they wouldn't have known about them. By revealing your weaknesses too openly, you run the risk of receiving criticism from others or perhaps being sued. And only once is it necessary. Alternatively, it might have been shown repeatedly just a decade earlier. Avoid becoming overly emotional and exposed.

As a result, even though it's become fashionable to be completely open about our flaws and concerns, be careful not to overexpose your weaknesses and be aware of the potential repercussions.

Also, be careful not to equate "vulnerability" with "emotionality." It's all too easy to expose our weaknesses when we're feeling vulnerable, only to feel a lot better about ourselves in the hours or days that follow once the emotion has passed. The damage has already been done by that point. We shared too much, and now we can't take it back.

Vulnerability has its proper time and place. In a stable emotional state, it's acceptable to be open and honest about your weaknesses in front of respected and qualified individuals. You should always ask for assistance when you need it.

But being overly open and vulnerable also restricts other people's regard for you, which diminishes your influence. Your reputation and integrity could be harmed.

Others will sway as you sway if they believe you to be weak and vulnerable. When you're terrified, other people will be as well.

The ability to be vulnerable has its place and time. It entails requesting the proper assistance from the proper sources. It's not about putting it in front of those who look to you for guidance and inspiration on social media or in front of everyone else.

Meetings, reviews, and leadership discussions don't include it. To your rivals or detractors, it most certainly is not.

Making Major decisions

Making firm or difficult judgments can become considerably more difficult when trying to "relate" to people by "being vulnerable." They think you're frail. You make it difficult for yourself to be strong right now. As a leader, you must inspire people to follow you. They must be capable of admiring and even respecting you. They must respect your tenacity and have faith in your capacity to overcome difficulties.

Too much open vulnerability sharing can give the impression that you are broken and helpless. People lose faith in your capacity to guide them through difficult and disruptive times.

I acknowledge that showing vulnerability may be a powerful way to connect with clients and foster trust. to establish a social media following and form relationships with the team and other employees.

However, I've discovered the hard way that being too transparent about my vulnerabilities with clients and employees undermines their faith in me and, consequently, in my teams. Others have used it as a tool for blackmail and manipulation.

Getting Over the Fear of Vulnerability.

It can be challenging to get over the vulnerability phobia, especially for individuals in leadership roles. Here are some tactics that could be useful:

PRACTICE SELF-AWARENESS

Start by developing a greater awareness of your own feelings, anxieties, and triggers. You can use this to pinpoint your most vulnerable regions and create a strategy for addressing them. Consider the advantages Remind yourself of the advantages of vulnerability in leadership, such as enhanced creativity, improved connections, and communication. You might be inspired to take the required actions to expose yourself to additional risk if you keep these advantages in mind.

Start Little

Start by being vulnerable in tiny ways, like telling a valued colleague a personal tale or owning up to a mistake at a team meeting. The degree of openness and honesty can be gradually increased as you gain confidence in your capacity to be vulnerable.

Accept Imperfections

Recognize that being vulnerable entails accepting imperfection and being prepared to display your human side. Keep in mind that learning from failure and making mistakes is a natural part of the process and that showing vulnerability can improve your leadership abilities.

Seek Assistance

Create a network of friends, mentors, and coworkers who will encourage you and be a source of feedback and guidance. As you work to become more vulnerable, this might make you feel more assured and supported.

Get Professional assistance

Seeking expert assistance, such as counseling or coaching, to work through these issues may be useful if you are battling ingrained concerns or trauma associated with vulnerability.

Keep in mind that developing leadership vulnerability is a process that requires time and effort. You can get past your anxieties and develop into a more genuine, sympathetic, and successful leader by being persistent, patient, and open to change.

Ways to Embrace and manage vulnerability.

1. *Admitting Mistakes*: Confess a mistake and discuss the takeaways from it.

2. *Sharing Personal Struggles*: Providing a safe space for open discussion on self-care while sharing struggles with work-life balance

3. *Asking for Assistance*: Be Humble, Value Team Members' Expertise, Admit Lack of Expertise, and Ask for Advice.

4. *Sharing Feedback*: Express any criticism you've received as a leader and pledge to work toward improvement.

5. *Conveying Uncertainty*: Convey uncertainty in the following steps of a difficult project.

6. *Demonstrating Empathy*: Recognize the emotional toll that a time of high stress can have, offer assistance, and promote open dialogue on mental health.

Chapter 3. Exhibiting Vulnerability and Courage

Although vulnerability and courage are frequently perceived as incompatible qualities, they are actually necessary for effective leadership. As a leader, you must be brave enough to take risks, make decisions, and inspire others while also being genuine, honest, and open to criticism. In this essay, you will discover how to develop these traits in yourself and your team.

The traits of strength and confidence are not weakness but vulnerability and courage. By acknowledging your mistakes and seeking assistance, these traits can help you, as a leader, develop trust and rapport with your team and stakeholders. By promoting experimentation, criticism, and failure, it can also promote a culture of learning and creativity. By taking on challenges, getting over concerns, and learning from failures, it can also increase resilience and adaptability. Additionally, it can increase influence and impact by communicating your goals, principles, and ideas as well as acting on them. Being true to yourself, your purpose, and your potential can also lead to greater satisfaction and fulfillment.

In the words of Jen Marr, "The minute you realize that Leadership is not about you, but of those you lead, you begin the process of vulnerability and courage".

Virtues of courage and vulnerability

Leaders must harness the power of courage and bravery to expose their vulnerability, identify the rationale for change, and communicate it transparently (Bahar Sedarati).

The ability to be vulnerable and courageous can be learned and cultivated, rather than being innate or fixed. Being self-aware and conscious of your strengths, flaws, emotions, and triggers will help you show vulnerability and courage as a leader. The importance of humility and curiosity about one's own and other people's perspectives, experiences, and needs cannot be overstated. It's also crucial to be open and truthful about your goals, objectives, and criticism.

It's crucial to support your team and other stakeholders while also recognizing their contributions and issues. Take calculated chances while being brave and determined in your goals, actions, and results. Last but not least, it's critical to take responsibility for your decisions, outcomes, and learning; the key is to acknowledge and absorb failure.

The pearls of courage and vulnerability

Since they are habits that must be developed and maintained, vulnerability and bravery are not one-time things. As a leader, you can ask for feedback and coaching from those who can encourage and test you, surround yourself with inspiring and motivating role models from all walks of life, celebrate accomplishments and recognize hard work, practice self-care and self-compassion to look after your physical, mental, and emotional wellbeing, and experiment with various ways of being and thinking while viewing uncertainty and change as opportunities.

Benefit of Exhibiting Courage and Vulnerability in Leadership

Leaders have always been viewed as those who take initiative and whose authority cannot (or should not) be questioned. However, the entire paradigm of leadership has been turned on its head as more generations enter the workforce with different expectations and ideals.

Today's leaders should be empathetic, courageous, and vulnerable rather than rigid and impervious. This frequently leads to better outcomes overall, closer relationships with their colleagues, and more productivity.

Manifesting Character Strength

Taking accountability for both ourselves and others is a requirement of leadership. A good leader can serve as an example if they can accept criticism, show their vulnerability, and recognize their mistakes while doing so. Owning our experiences and being vulnerable indicate character strength and emotional intelligence, two qualities that are crucial for leaders.

Increasing Trust

Genuine people are trusted by others. Without trust, customers do not remain devoted supporters, and staff do not remain at organizations for long. Regardless of the size or sector of the business, being vulnerable and keeping things "real" is crucial for effective leadership. It affects both interpersonal and professional connections.

Making You Relatable

In order to be a true leader, a person must be inspired and inspire others inside the company. However, it's also crucial for the people under the leader to be able to relate to the leader. Their relatability and resulting stronger emotional connection are facilitated by their vulnerability.

Motivating Creativity

Cultures of creativity and greater involvement are inspired by leaders who accept their insecurities, whether they are making mistakes or having trouble coming up with a solution. Employee productivity and loyalty are increased since it allows them space to unwind and pursue personal and professional development in a friendly setting.

Achieving Consistent Growth

Being vulnerable will enable you to grow immensely, in addition to giving your colleagues the impression that you are more approachable and human. Being vulnerable enables us to consider possibilities and solutions that we would not have otherwise considered. The team will be able to contribute meaningfully and will feel more appreciated by the organization if the leader acknowledges they don't have all the answers.

Psychological safety promotion

Teams that feel psychologically safe perform better than those that don't, according to research by Harvard Business School professor Amy C. Edmondson. When a leader demonstrates vulnerability, it invites followers to do the same. This could contribute to creating the culture of trust that high-performing teams need.

Molds You Into A Contemporary Leader

Accepting vulnerability fosters trust, which is the cornerstone of any successful business partnership. Leaders who demonstrate vulnerability and courage often evolve into the types of modern leaders that people love to work for and with. Tactical managers may still hide behind unassailable power, but the greatest leaders I've worked for have done both.

Authenticity as a Bridge to Connection

You don't have to be correct all the time to be a genuine leader. Both leaders and the teams they lead are made up of people. You'll be able to connect with your team on a deeper level by being vulnerable and real. Human nature dictates that people can tell when a leader is being genuine. Being genuine will inspire teams and increase your chances of success.

Getting Other People to Help

Leaders run the risk of alienating themselves and losing touch with their team if they come across as infallible and always right. By being vulnerable, employers encourage their staff to share both their ideas and their issues in an effort to improve every part of the company. Vulnerability invites anyone, not just coworkers, to assist and participate.

Being emotional does not equate to being vulnerable. Being vulnerable as a leader requires being truthful with both yourself and others. You can acknowledge when you don't have all the solutions and when you need assistance. This fosters trust between you and your team and can result in some of the strongest professional relationships.

Chapter 4: Bravery in Leadership.

Ethical, moral, and legal behavior is required of brave leaders. It is not leadership to follow another person blindly just because they are higher up in the chain of command. No one has the authority to agree to every request or judgment simply because they have a title. Leaders are courageous enough to defend their convictions and refuse opportunities that can be risky or unethical. They also know when it's time to query choices that can endanger the wellbeing of their team members or organization.

Not all bravery involves adopting a position. It also has to do with how we act toward other people. It helps the team manage challenging situations when there is a little sympathy. Small acts of kindness and setting a good example provide others with the skills they need to tackle their own problems in life and at work.

Guidelines for brave leadership in action

Many executives find it difficult to acknowledge situations beyond their control. That shouldn't be shocking. Years have been spent teaching them that leaders should "be strong." We may and ought to challenge the veracity of their convictions. However, this does not alter the fact that leaders always have to make challenging choices. The fact that leaders must always make difficult choices, however, is unaffected by this. Both their businesses and the people they lead are guided by these choices.

However, leadership goes beyond what we do. It also has to do with what we don't do. Honesty makes leaders better when they take a step back and acknowledge that they cannot control the outcome. It takes courage to choose to be honest.

In keeping with that, we're offering five guidelines for courageous leadership "in the wild." We sincerely hope that doing so will increase your leadership bravery.

Even when it's uncomfortable, brave leaders communicate with their teams.

We are aware that asking difficult questions might be challenging. Giving constructive criticism and avoiding awkward conversations with your team are both more comfortable. But courageous leaders don't let their very human desire to be liked stand in the way of doing their jobs.

Leadership is about having the courage to take risks. to deliver bad news, push back when a team member becomes irritable, or discuss a direct report's subpar performance. Even though it's unpleasant, courageous leaders have these difficult dialogues. They are aware that this is part of their duties. In light of this, what conversation can you have today that you've been putting off even though it's necessary for you to do so as a leader?

STRONG LEADERS ARE ACCOUNTABLE FOR THEIR CHOICES AND RESULTS.

A lot of leaders enjoy being in the spotlight. Success, however, not only resulted in prestige but also difficulty. When leaders make mistakes, their failures become public affairs because they are in the spotlight. Risk-taking leaders hold themselves accountable when their risks don't produce the expected outcomes.

The President of the United States, Teddy Roosevelt, believed in holding oneself accountable and admitting his own leadership flaws and mistakes. Regarding his shortcomings, he observed, "If you could kick the person in the pants who is most responsible for most of your trouble, you wouldn't sit for a month."

Roosevelt was aware that many of the biggest barriers to one's own performance are ones that one has put in place; failing to acknowledge these barriers would have a negative impact on the effectiveness of people under his supervision. In the same vein, courageous leaders are prepared to take accountability for their deeds, including their failures. Are you avoiding taking responsibility for your deeds or blaming others when you fail?

COURAGEOUS LEADERS IMPROVE OTHERS UNCERTAIN LEADERS WORRY ABOUT LOSING THEIR POSITION.

On the other hand, courageous leaders are aware of their responsibilities to uphold the organization's values and make it possible for others to contribute to its success. They are there to empower others, not to exercise their own authority. to listen more than you talk and to have empathy. rather than relying solely on their own authority, to learn from their underlings and hand up the reins. To create rules and define values, but to leave it up to their team to put those into practice and build on them.

Returning to Matthew McCarthy, he succinctly encapsulated this idea in his explanation of why senior leaders at businesses must step back and let younger team members take the reins on The Hidden Edge of Team Performance podcast: "A zombie can be carried for a very long time by the momentum of our markets."

Courageous leaders protest injustice.

Leaders must be prepared to stand up for fundamental beliefs when they are disregarded by followers or buried beneath organizational politics. Because they would rather blend in with their coworkers and avoid endangering their positions of power and privilege, those who lack bravery choose to remain mute in the face of injustice or wrongdoing. But courageous leaders will defend their principles even if it means risking their reputation or their livelihood.

What ideals are you prepared to defend and uphold, even at the risk of suffering consequences?

COURAGEOUS LEADERS PRACTICE WHAT THEY PREACH.

Cowards make grand statements but take no action. Contrarily, daring leaders invest in the initiatives they support because they think they will advance the organization and the individuals that make it up. Avoid falling for this trap. Put your money where your mouth is and do the effort. Check your ego at the door, put aside blatant self-promotion, and do whatever is necessary to achieve the goal. You are a force. Use it, then. responsibly and in the interest of your mission and your people.

Ask yourself: What important endeavor can I support to help it succeed by putting my full support behind it? How can my team and I work together more freely, vocally, and effectively to attain this goal? What brave resource reallocation can I sway to ensure this favorable outcome—not for myself but for the entire organization?

Be a brave leader. Your group will comply.

Seven Eccentricities Of Daring Leaders

These are tense and unsettled times. the kind of circumstances that compelled our forefathers to raise the drawbridge, fortify themselves, and take precautions. Very secure. a result of fear. It prevents people from acting in a way that would ultimately increase their long-term success. We need strong leaders to display true courage at times when people are gazing up at the sky and wondering when it will collapse.

The kind of bravery that can tell actual risks from imagined ones and doesn't minimize the cost of being indecisive in the face of uncertainty. the kind that motivates individuals to get together in support of an admirable cause and admit what isn't working. the kind that doesn't rely on terror to compel behavior, gather support, secure votes, or demean those who differ. the kind that encourages innovative thinking and makes use of all available skills, knowledge, and talent.

A necessary condition for truly outstanding leadership is courage. Although it can take various forms, the determination to act in the face of uncertainty, to choose what is right over what is expedient, and to run the risk of failing and falling short in the process are the core characteristics of courageous leadership. Why? Because no amount of genius or showmanship will be enough unless leaders are prepared to risk their psychological safety (i.e., pride and power) for the benefit of those they serve.

But let's face it, more people would adopt change and act decisively in the face of uncertainty if it were simple to do so. Our minds are programmed to seek security and safety rather than taking chances. That they lived too safely and took too few risks is one of the biggest regrets of the dying, which is not surprising. It is no wonder we are currently experiencing such a lack of courageous leadership.

It takes a strong "Why" to reach deep inside of yourself and summon the confidence to move past the emotion of fear. Practice these seven traits of daring leaders if you're serious about standing out from the crowd. Why not you, since we require more of them? Anyone with the courage to lead with it may exercise real leadership; it is not just reserved for those with stellar credentials.

Courageous leaders create a bold vision.

Brave visionaries make for brave leaders. They may have to operate in the world of probabilities, but they take the initiative in the domain of possibilities because they are aware that we often fail because we are too frightened to take risks. Think about Elon Musk. Compared to most people, he has experienced more failures. ones that are widely publicized and excite his detractors. However, Musk's audacious vision for what is possible has brought together some of the world's best minds to break new ground and push the limits of possibility, whether in space with Space X or on the roads in a Tesla. Leaders with guts know to distinguish between what has never been done before and what is actually impossible.

Courageous leaders seek out critics and promote inclusion.

Brave leaders don't surround themselves with yes men' (or women) who will support their beliefs and tickle their egos (and don't terminate people who do!). Instead, they look for individuals whose viewpoints and perspectives will differ from and broaden their own. And once they locate them, They engage in active listening and foster the psychological safety necessary for individuals with less influence to express their disagreements and talk openly. Accordingly, they deliberately promote an inclusive workplace so that individuals who don't fit the norm feel just as respected and heard as those who do, in addition to valuing diversity in their teams and networks across gender, ethnic, cultural, generational, and personality lines.

Brave leaders defy the norm.

Brave leaders are nonconformists who frequently break away from the system to challenge the conventions and ideas that underpin it because they are aware of the risks associated with untested assumptions. A good example of this is Richard Branson. Many American CEOs, many of whom have never taken more than two weeks off consecutively in their whole careers, shook their heads when he instituted unlimited leave for Virgin America staff.

A person is free to tour the world for a month if they so desire. When they return, they will put forth even more effort. At the Adobe Summit, Branson questioned America's typical 2–3 weeks of annual vacation and claimed that it had little effect on the company. "Treating people with flexibility, as fellow humans, and as you would treat your own children has a significant positive impact on the company."

Courageous Leaders Speak Honestly While Considering Others' needs.

The most detrimental effects on employee engagement, individual performance, and group outcomes can result from avoiding unpleasant talks, which is why courageous leaders don't avoid them. It may feel comfortable in the short run to only express what is safe (or what other people want to hear), but beware the long-term costs of ignoring critical topics. Chances are, if there is anything you truly need to say, someone else truly needs to hear it.

Bold leaders make decisions despite ambiguity.

A leader who is courageous will make a courageous decision. They understand that waiting until they can eliminate all risk and have complete confidence would be a waste of time. Instead, they do their research and crunch the numbers before reaching the best decision they can. And when they have a "miss-step," they instantly own it and change their direction. What they don't do is wait until they are positive they won't make a mistake before proceeding. Therefore, do not let your fear of making a poor choice prevent you from choosing wisely. The cost of delay rises steadily.

Courageous leaders increase trust Delegators, not micromanagers, are brave leaders.

They concentrate on the areas where they contribute the most value and let others handle the rest, restricting their supervision to what is required to make sure that each person's activities are consistent with those of the group. Despite their want to assist, they resist the impulse to step in and handle other people's difficulties and instead let them work out their own solutions. People typically live up to the amount of expectation placed on them, according to study. If you treat them as unreliable and in need of continual supervision, that is what you will get.

Treat them as capable individuals who have the capacity to learn and succeed, and you'll also get that. Therefore, resist the need to withhold your trust from others out of a concern that they won't perform as well as you do or that they might make a mistake and reflect poorly on you. Aim high, and you'll achieve it. Expecting little will also get you that. Put your faith in others to go above and beyond your expectations.

Courageous leaders encourage followers to take risks.

When they feel unsafe, people take safety precautions. Risk aversion is fueled when leaders concentrate on the negative effects of failure. It is for this reason that courageous leaders deliberately attempt to foster a "culture of courage," in which individuals are encouraged to speak up, confront conventional wisdom, try out novel concepts, take calculated risks, and put growth and contribution before safety and comfort. And if things don't go as expected, They make kind assumptions in order to take advantage of the shared learning and "fail forward" as a group.

There is ultimately no shortcut to developing the guts required to be an empowering, motivating, and effective leader. Beginning with the following choice you must make, you create it gradually. In readiness? Accept discomfort, believe in your abilities, and don't let fear rule your decisions. Nothing genuinely remarkable is accomplished without courage, according to Dr. Margie Warrell. However, acting courageously does not ensure your success.

Chapter 5: Reasons For Failure in Leadership and Navigating up

No one should underestimate the responsibility that comes with leadership. Numerous things, such as a leader's lack of experience, poor communication abilities, and disagreements with other leaders, can contribute to leadership failure. To avoid losing the trust of those around them or jeopardizing their authority as a leader, leaders must always put their best foot forward.

Everyone in business, including managers and leaders, has strengths and weaknesses. Being a leader comes with the additional duty of identifying your areas of weakness and strengthening them to help your team more effectively. You'll be more motivated to use the finest leadership techniques for your team if you have a better understanding of why leadership fails.

Failure in leadership is inevitable. It's challenging to prevent it at any time in any business. Even if you are the most skilled leader, you could occasionally be viewed as impatient.

Everyone in business, including managers and leaders, has strengths and weaknesses. Being a leader comes with the additional duty of identifying your areas of weakness and strengthening them to help your team more effectively. You'll be more motivated to use the finest leadership techniques for your team if you have a better understanding of why.

In this article, we list some of the major variables that might undermine a leader's effectiveness and describe how to reroute them into constructive actions.

long-term team development and team building.

Here are some typical reasons for poor leadership, along with solutions you can implement at work:

1. Focus on the individual

Too much individualism can lead to unsuccessful leadership because strong leaders understand the value of working as a team. Productivity and morale may suffer if one person's priorities take precedence over the team as a whole. Leading and inspiring a team requires promoting both teamwork and individual success.

Avoid bias when acting as a leader and encourage teamwork by recognizing and giving everyone on the team an equal chance at success. Consider the value that each role brings to the group while highlighting the advantages of cooperation. To motivate everyone on the team to excel in their roles and help others, share the benefits of successful initiatives with them.

2. BOREDOM AND IDLENESS

Passionate about what they do, transformational leaders use their enthusiasm to motivate others. It may be more difficult for leaders to inspire their team and themselves when they are bored or idle at work. It is much simpler to persuade others to follow your leadership when you are invested in your work and have a promising outlook for the future.

To inspire your team and foster a love of any subject, consider the long-term advantages and effects of every work you do. To avoid monotony and discover moments of pleasure and happiness to share with your team, look for growth possibilities, take chances, and employ new ways in your work.

3. Inconsistent Communication

Since effective teamwork depends on effective communication, the way you communicate as a leader has a big impact on how well you lead. You must communicate your expectations for the team to every member of the team in a consistent and understandable manner. Increase productivity by periodically gathering your team, both individually and collectively, to discuss goals and go over any changes to the workplace.

By using both verbal and written communication to share performance goals and document best practices for completing tasks, you may eliminate confusion in your role as a leader. Encourage your staff by complimenting their good work and offering meaningful, constructive criticism to help them develop their abilities. Support two-way communication by giving your team a way to offer advice on how you can improve as a leader.

4. DISORGANIZATION

A leadership position requires juggling several tasks and priorities at once. You can struggle to manage your tasks and keep your promises to your team if you don't have a robust organizational framework in place. Putting organization first can help you manage your time better and give you more time and energy to work with your team.

Utilize tools like spreadsheets, timetables, calendars, timelines, and reminder notifications to practice being more organized. Schedule time each week to complete your personal tasks and communicate with your colleagues about important goals. You might experience a better ability to support your team members when you manage your time well, plan your tasks, and allocate your resources.

5 Micromanagement

Influential leaders strike a balance between taking the initiative to finish tasks and having faith in their team's abilities. Your team will miss out on possibilities for progress if you micromanage their assignments, and it will take up a lot of your time. As a leader, if you take on too many duties, you could become overburdened and unintentionally sabotage processes.

Establish checkpoint meetings to examine the status of projects with your team and do away with micromanagement. This gives everyone on the team the opportunity to contribute and use their talents while also providing adequate oversight to address problems.

6. Inappropriate Accountability

As a leader, you are accountable for the results of your team's efforts. If a leader takes credit for their team's accomplishments but holds them responsible for difficulties, leadership may fail. Being responsible as a leader fosters trust among team members and demonstrates your commitment to their success.

Show your team that you are accountable by being focused and disciplined in your work. Setting a good example for the team motivates them to take responsibility for their contributions to the project. Recognize how you wish to get better so you can provide greater results the next time the team faces difficulties. Request suggestions from the team on how to support them further, then describe your plans for putting those ideas into action.

7. A DEARTH OF RESEARCH

The principles of their profession are strong, and great leaders are aware of their surroundings. You may provide your team with additional advice that is more pertinent by doing research and learning about the procedures and best practices in your sector.

Use your team as a resource to avoid letting a lack of sector expertise affect your leadership style. To learn more, ask them to impart their expertise in the area to you or arrange mutual mentoring sessions. Make plans for the team's ongoing professional development training opportunities, and make notes on any subjects you want to research more on your own.

8. Failure to adapt

Being adaptable and innovative are key components of visionary leadership. Leaders risk missing possibilities for development and success if they insist on employing the same strategies and tactics. Your team will be able to create a long-term career under your direction if you pay attention to their innovative proposals and adapt to your environment.

Attend conferences, learn about business trends, and keep an eye out for workplace trends to avoid office stagnation. Reward those that contribute original thinking and are open to trying out fresh approaches to achieving objectives.

9. A Depressing Perspective

Whether it's a good or bad impact, your attitude as a leader affects everyone around you. Team members may become aware of a leader's pessimistic view and gradually begin to adopt it for their own work. Create positive behaviors and an upbeat attitude on purpose to avoid problems with team morale.

Try encouraging positivity by giving your team members frequent compliments and expressing your enthusiasm for their job. Use uplifting rhetoric and provide solutions while talking about difficult subjects. Instead of critiquing others, concentrate on being positive about making improvements.

10. Vague objectives

Leading a team is difficult when you're unaware of the objectives you wish to achieve. Team members rely on leaders to set important goals and create a strategy for accomplishing them. Setting clear objectives for yourself and your group will direct your leadership efforts, allow you to monitor your success, and make it simpler to spot problems.

Establish a baseline for productivity using information from previous projects completed by your team, then pinpoint areas for improvement. Include a schedule for when you anticipate each team member to complete each goal when you list a few specific goals for them to concentrate on. To help the team stay motivated, post the goals somewhere convenient and visible.

11. Unrealistic Expectations

Lack of goals can lead to leadership problems, but having too rigid goals might demoralize the team. Make sure your goals are reasonable and reachable based on the knowledge, expertise, and effort that each member of your team can bring to the table. Start with simple goals and work your way up to long-term changes to help your team flourish.

Identify if a goal is feasible for your team by reviewing industry standards and past productivity levels. Schedule conversations with your team to discuss their workload and how they feel about attempting team goals. Make goals more realistic by providing your team with professional development resources and mentoring them to improve their efficiency.

Effective leadership

To be an effective leader, Examine industry norms and previous productivity levels to determine whether a target is doable for your team. Plan meetings with your team to talk about their workload and how they feel about pursuing team objectives. By offering your team opportunities for professional growth and coaching them to increase efficiency, you can make goals more achievable.

One of the most crucial requirements for a highly engaged, coordinated, productive, and empowered staff is effective leadership.

Additionally, leadership is crucial to creating a better workplace culture and a great employee experience. For the rest of the team, leaders should set an example by living up to the fundamental principles of the organization. These suggestions can help you develop your leadership abilities whether you are just starting out or have been managing teams for some time. These mentioned secrets are used by leaders with a track record of success.

Expansion

Two of the most crucial areas to concentrate on when developing into a good leader are:

- *Ownership of purpose*
- *Financial expertise*

Owning your purpose entails having a distinct vision for what you want to do and then accepting full accountability for carrying it out. To achieve this, you must have well-defined objectives, be enthusiastic about your work, and be dedicated to ongoing personal and professional development.

Financial mastery, on the other hand, revolves around knowing how money functions and how to take advantage of it. This entails cultivating wise financial practices, making investments in your career and business, and continuously exploring for income-boosting opportunities.

You can position yourself for both personal and professional success by concentrating on these two crucial areas.

Put together a motivated team.

Without a strong team supporting them, no leader can achieve success. You'll be well on your way to being a top-tier leader if you put together a team of committed individuals with complementary skill sets to support your vision.

The strongest teams are those that value communication, respect, and trust. Make sure to create a space where people can express their ideas and opinions without feeling awkward. Additionally, always be ready to listen to others; this will help you win their respect.

When you put up a united front, the sky's the limit!

Over Communicate

According to an old adage, "If you want something done, ask a busy person to do it." Successful leaders could also be compared to this.

Effective communication is crucial for team and organizational leadership. Yet so many managers fail to grasp the significance of excessive communication. They believe that their employees will automatically "get it" and that they won't need to go into great depth to explain things.

The opposite is true, as you can see. *Successful leaders are aware that details are frequently the key to effective communication.*

Leaders may make sure that their team is on the same page and that everyone is aware of what has to be done by communicating excessively. In the long run, this not only saves time but also lessens confusion and misunderstandings.

Avoid assuming.

Never assume that a great leader knows everything. They are always eager to pick up new skills and hear what others have to say. They are able to consistently advance their leadership qualities and capabilities due to their willingness to try new concepts and methods. Great leaders can also encourage and inspire others to do their best work. They can aid others in realizing their potential by leading by example and giving clear instructions.

Be sincere

CEO responsibilities are undoubtedly challenging. However, effective leaders are aware that success and authenticity go hand in hand.

It is insufficient to merely show up and perform your duties. To gain your team's respect and trust, you must be sincere, open, and honest with them. This entails being honest about your errors, outlining your company's goals, and fostering a culture where people feel free to express their opinions.

People are more inclined to trust you and your leadership when you are real. They'll be more invested in the success of your business and more committed to its mission. Therefore, start by being yourself if you want to become a CEO who leaves a lasting impression.

Recognize your challenges

Great leaders are aware of their challenges and frequently work with coaches or mentors to help them get through them. According to best-selling book and leadership expert John C. Maxwell, "a leader is one who knows the way, goes the way, and shows the way." You must first recognize your challenges if you want to be a great leader. When you are aware of the obstacles in your path, you may start to create a strategy to overcome them. It can be quite beneficial to have a mentor or coach as you seek to develop your leadership abilities.

These people can help you as you work to realize your full potential by providing advice and encouragement. The opportunities are endless when you make the decision to develop into a great leader. In order to get started, understand more about your challenges and ask for assistance from individuals who can aid you along the way. It's time to put your abilities to work so that you can succeed.

Construct a team charter

Success for leaders can be aided by developing a team charter. The mission, roles, and obligations of the team are outlined in the charter. Additionally, it establishes guidelines for how the team will function as a whole. A team's effectiveness and efficiency can be increased by a well-written charter.

The following considerations should guide leaders as they draft a team charter:

1. Specify the goal for the group.

2. Delegate jobs and duties.

3. Specify the standards by which workers are to interact.

4. Specify the parameters of the group's success.

5. Write a brief document that everyone can comprehend and accept.

A team charter is a useful tool for managers to create and keep winning teams. By spending the effort to draft a charter, leaders can make sure that their team has a unified mission and purpose. Teams may be able to operate more productively and effectively as a result, which will eventually produce better outcomes.

Trust your people (Staffs).

Strong executives have faith in their workforce. They are aware that their staff members have the knowledge and skills necessary to complete the task successfully. These leaders are aware that in order for their staff to succeed, they need to provide guidance and direction. Through successful communication, they offer this advice and direction. Clear and explicit expectations are communicated by strong executives. In order to make sure that their staff members are on track, they also periodically provide feedback. Strong executives foster an environment where their staff members can flourish by taking these actions.

Assign credit

Giving credit where credit is due is crucial. *By doing this, you demonstrate your fairness and appreciation for others' contributions.*

Giving someone credit makes a strong statement about how much you value their work. This, in turn, may inspire them to keep putting in hard work and supporting the squad.

There will undoubtedly be instances where you must refuse credit in the interest of the group or the business. Giving credit where credit is due, however, will go a long way toward fostering a climate of mutual respect and trust among your team members.

Maintain team enthusiasm

An effective leader knows how to maintain the team's interest. They may maximize the potential of their team by motivating and communicating effectively. They also understand how to foster an environment at work where everyone is recognized and appreciated.

They have a higher propensity to go above and beyond for their employer and a lower propensity to change jobs. A successful firm will be run by a leader who can keep their workforce motivated.

Compliments and gratitude

A great leader exhibits wisdom in both their words and deeds and is skilled at conveying praise and gratitude. They are also adept at celebrating success in a way that motivates others.

Remain composed.

When you're stressed out, it might be challenging to maintain your composure. But being able to maintain composure is crucial if you want to be a good leader. Otherwise, you run the risk of making judgments based more on feelings than reason.

So how can powerful leaders maintain their composure? by putting a plan in place. They are able to pinpoint the source of their stress and have a strategy in place to cope with it.

Chapter 6: Leadership accountability

Accepting responsibility for your work's outcomes, regardless of success, is the act of being accountable. Accountability as a leader can strengthen their relationship with their team members because it encourages practicing honesty. No matter where you work, becoming a stronger leader can be facilitated by learning more about accountable leadership.

Accountable leadership

When a department's executives assume accountability for the outcomes of their actions, this is known as accountable leadership. A good example of an accountable leader is one that accepts the outcomes of a marketing campaign they managed, regardless of whether they fulfill expectations. Developing an accountable culture where staff members feel appreciated and valued is facilitated by accountable leadership practices.

Highly responsible leaders set excellent models for those they supervise and could promote employee responsibility. With accountable leadership, leaders are held accountable for their own behavior as well as their treatment of subordinates. This promotes employee transparency and aids in maintaining corporate transparency.

While leaders must hold themselves accountable for company objectives, it's equally critical to foster accountability for people and culture. Lack of accountability may have a negative effect on business culture or employee morale, yet strong organizational accountability fosters productive workplaces.

Positive effects of responsible leadership Organizations need accountable leaders to keep them moving in the right direction. By fostering trust and a supportive, accountable workplace culture, they can retain staff members committed to the company's objectives. Employees who are held accountable may feel more a part of the organization and its leadership group. A few more advantages of accountable leadership are as follows:

increased trust

By taking responsibility for their actions, departmental leaders can foster a sense of trust among their team members. Because each action receives the proper response from leaders, accountability fosters confidence. Employees should expect to be recognized for their contributions and any noteworthy job they complete, for instance, if their leader upholds high standards for accountability. Because accountability reduces blame-shifting and ensures employees receive credit for their work, which increases trust between employees and leaders.

Improved relationships

Accountability in leadership can help strengthen relationships within a department or business. If a leader takes accountability for a large project within a marketing department, regardless of the success or potential failure of the project, employees can work without worrying about project accountability issues. Similarly, if each employee is accountable for parts of a large project, this ensures less confusion surrounding allocating responsibilities. With less worry and confusion about workplace responsibilities, employee relationships improve and develop throughout a project's duration.

Accountability lowers finger-pointing and ensures workers get credit for their contributions, which boosts trust between workers and leaders.

Enhanced connections

Accountability in management can improve connections within a team or organization. Employees can operate without being concerned about project accountability problems if a leader accepts responsibility for a significant project within a marketing department, regardless of the project's success or possible failure. Similar to this, if each person is responsible for a portion of a big project, there will be less confusion about who is responsible for what. Throughout the course of a project, employee connections deepen and develop since there is less concern and uncertainty regarding duties at work.

Reduced error rates

Achieving accountable leadership reduces errors made during the process. Even though it's hard to completely avoid errors, you can reduce the likelihood of errors by making sure everyone is aware of their responsibilities. As a result, those who accept responsibility for their mistakes can acquire training, enroll in courses, and find opportunities to hone their abilities over time, which can further improve mistake minimization.

Techniques to develop into a responsible leader

To become more responsible, there are various strategies to improve your leadership abilities. While some abilities come naturally, many leaders train themselves to carry out particular tasks in order to be responsible for their work and team members. Consider using the following strategies if you want to learn how to be a responsible leader at work:

MAKE GOALS CLEAR.

Clarity includes outlining the objective and the significance of it. Clarifying project goals is one step you may take to become a more accountable leader. Setting up clear objectives and the routes to achieving them makes it simpler for people to take responsibility for various activities. You and other staff members can become more accountable if you continue to be transparent about every facet of a goal..

Concentrate on the future.

By concentrating on the department's future, you may further your efforts to promote responsibility. Knowing where the department is headed and how it will get there is one of your responsibilities as a leader. Planning these aspects enables you to be more accountable for your duties and demonstrates to your team that you are capable of handling them. Accountability entails not only taking accountability for previous deeds but also making responsible plans for future deeds.

Get Feedback.

Getting feedback as frequently as you can is one strategy to increase accountability as a leader. You can maintain responsibility for your obligations by listening to employee feedback. Employee comments about your actions will help you prepare even more for the following project if they see that you finished the things on your agenda. Your goals can be adjusted with the use of feedback, which can also show you when a goal regularly benefits the department.

Offer sincere Feedback.

Giving sincere feedback as frequently as you can is another step you can take to establish yourself as a responsible leader. Giving your staff feedback based on their duties at work can encourage them to continue taking responsibility for their work in the future. The team may learn more about their development and produce greater results with honest feedback. Employees can learn to improve the quality of their work over time while accepting responsibility for their actions by regularly giving honest criticism and encouraging constant accountability.

Accept responsibility for mistakes and accomplishments.

Accepting your accomplishments and failings as a leader is one way to maintain accountability. Employees are more likely to view your job in an honest light when you accept both good and bad performance from yourself.

When speaking about matters pertaining to the organization, use "we" instead of "I" to encourage this type of accountability from everyone. Equal responsibility for your own acts creates justice, fosters accountability within your department, and shows excellent accountability to others.

BECOME MINDFUL OF YOUR WORKLOAD.

Workload awareness should be practiced as frequently as feasible if you want to become a more accountable leader. The department's overall work accountability can be improved by knowing how much work you and others can handle at certain times of the year. Leaders must be accountable in several ways, including only taking on tasks they can finish. If you assign your work to another employee because you are unable to do it yourself, this can demonstrate that you are aware of your limitations and have faith in your colleague to get the job done.

MAKE SURE COMMUNICATION IS EFFICIENT.

As a responsible leader, make improvements to your communication strategies to promote a pleasant workplace culture. To ensure that subjects are discussed in the right environment, you might establish a variety of communication channels. A leader should think about supporting open communication as much as possible in addition to providing staff with more opportunities for communication. Maintaining accountability for certain goals and encouraging accountability among team members can both be accomplished through open communication.

SET OBJECTIVES BASED ON THE ABILITIES OF THE SQUAD.

Understanding the talents of your team will help you be more accountable as a leader.

Allocating those jobs to other staff is the best course of action if you can't reasonably complete them within a set amount of time. However, assigning tasks to workers necessitates in-depth familiarity with team skills. Knowing what each member of your team is capable of indicates your familiarity with their skills.

Understanding each employee's capabilities and present goals will help you both stay accountable for the work you assign to them. You can assign jobs more effectively if you know their preferences for the work. By doing this, you may demonstrate to your team that you are aware of their abilities, which will help you reach your goals more rapidly.

Hold numerous meetings.

Hosting numerous meetings is another way that a leader can ensure accountability. Regular meetings allow you to review current goals, go over incomplete projects, and explain requirements. Each employee can review their tasks during meetings to see if task distribution is an option. Meeting minutes that document progress can be used to organize performance reviews, provide answers to inquiries, and provide fresh perspectives on project advances. By regularly checking in on each other's work, you are embracing responsibility for your own actions as well as the team's performance.

ENCOURAGE TRYING NEW THINGS.

Encourage experimentation and original thought as techniques to improve leadership abilities. Teams learn to accept responsibility for experimental gain and risk when given the freedom to play within a project's constraints. Encouragement of experimentation unintentionally encourages frequent communication between team members, leaders, and other workers because experimenting necessitates communication within a team.

Chapter 7: Delivering Impactful Leadership

Employing a framework to choose, evaluate, and improve their leaders' abilities and competences is necessary to guarantee that leaders are in line with the business impact that organizations seek to achieve. Making decisions, setting priorities, and aligning leaders with the organization's values, objectives, and aspirations can all be done with the support of the Leading With Impact Framework.

According to a quote by Orison Swett Marden, *"There are powers inside of you that, if you could discover and use them, would make you everything you ever dreamed or imagined you could become."*

Making a personal impact means evolving into your best self, someone who the organization will gravitate toward and have an influence on. It derives from both your internal and external behaviors. Change-makers, innovators, and successful influencers can successfully inspire others to achieve greater success.

Your capacity to establish personal credibility, be trustworthy, manage adversity, lead change, forge strong connections, grow in self-awareness, and lead with your core values in mind is the foundation of your leadership excellence.

If people don't believe they can trust you, it's easy to lose credibility. Openly complaining, spreading rumors, hiding information, telling lies that are only partially true, acting arrogantly, or refusing to accept criticism from others are all mistakes that undermine a leader's credibility and influence.

It's crucial to consider whether the actions you take every day help build credibility and trust among your team members. Accept responsibility for your actions, admit when you've erred in judgment or made a mistake, and only commit to things you can actually keep.

Adversity and resistance are encountered by all leaders on occasion. You must constantly remind yourself to be adaptable and upbeat about the future. At all times, you serve as an example for your team, and when you act positively, they are more likely to be motivated to do the same.

Self-awareness and emotional intelligence are required to anticipate the effects of your emotional reactions to difficult events on other people. Ask for input on your personal strengths and shortcomings, be aware of your limitations, and take aggressive steps to get past them.

In order to leave a personal leadership legacy, you must be a capable, respectable business leader in your industry while also adhering to your core values and ideals. Make certain that your choices and actions are consistent with the kind of person you hope to become. You ought to be able to articulate the connection between your actions and the things that are most important to you. No matter how many procedures and policies are in place, there is simply no alternative to letting your basic beliefs and values direct your behavior.Live by your own personal code of conduct to be a successful leader with personal influence.

If you can express what is most important to you and respect the differences among the team members, you will be better able to develop a strong and dedicated team. You have the ability to persuade people to reach new heights.

Because leadership qualities are crucial for success in a functional leadership job, a competent leader is one who has influence. These leadership skills include

1 *Executive communication.* Clearly communicates ideas and makes use of language to foster understanding.

Performance and outcomes Aligns resources to achieve essential goals and establishes clear accountability for those goals. achieves significant successes. Persuasion encourages and inspires others to act.

2 **Strategic Viewpoint.** A strategic viewpoint enables leaders gain perspective and resolve the conflict between routine duties and important strategic decisions that affect the organization's long-term sustainability

5. **Crossing boundaries.** This builds cooperative partnerships across the organization. Commitment inspires people to give their best effort.

7: **Comprehending the Business.** It requires a thorough understanding of the organization's conditions and the viewpoints of the various functional areas. possesses both depth and breadth of experience.

8: **Vision.** Comprehends, articulates, and maintains attention on the organization's vision.

9 *Invention*. Integrates information, viewpoints, and methods to invent, produce stronger results, and produce greater value.

10: *Approachability and executive presence*. Builds relationships by being approachable and visible. demonstrates friendliness and humor.

11 *Self-knowledge*. Have a precise understanding of the value they provide and a comprehensive understanding of their strengths and growth requirements.

12: *Learning flexibility*. Broadens one's options for learning through experience is growth-oriented.

13 *A global leader*. Understands how to lead and conduct business globally.

REQUIRED APPROACH TO LEAD WITH IMPACT

Functional leaders may sharpen their focus and increase performance in ways that will have a significant impact. The functional leaders that are most successful adopt a more focused strategy. They manage the pressure of "everything is important" and maintain their attention on the leadership competencies that are most crucial to their organization. We offer the following advice for functional leaders:

REQUEST INPUT. Seek candid feedback on what's most important and how other people perceive you as a capable leader in the absence of a formal assessment. Pay particular attention to variations in levels.

IDENTIFY PROBLEMS. Clarify the leadership issues you currently face or will experience in the upcoming years.

Establish what's most crucial. **Think about the leadership changes that would have the biggest impact. Start with the leadership skills that seem to match the issues you are facing. Consider what you could learn or do better when you examine the competencies associated with one of your main issue areas. Concentrate on the skill that will be most valuable to your organization if you develop it. Be mindful of any variations in what your supervisor, peers, and superiors might find valuable.**

Investigate and learn. **Look for new roles that will expand your experience both broadly and deeply. Innovation and global leadership are particularly important for the success of global organizations. Ask for assistance.**

CONCLUSION

Leadership development is the process by which a professional improves their abilities and traits to become a more powerful leader. Professionals concentrate on specific categories—often referred to as leadership development areas—to achieve this. Knowing which areas to concentrate on may be helpful if you want to improve your leadership potential.

This book provides advice and examples to serve as a guide while covering important leadership development topics and their respective importance.

A corporation may achieve its targeted goals and ensure that both managers and employees are performing to their full capacity by having strong leaders within the management team. Knowing where each leader needs to grow can help produce stronger managers and foster efficiency and optimism at work.

You might become a stronger leader by prioritizing your growth and identifying areas in which you need to grow as a leader. While self-reflection and deliberate behavior change can address these issues, there are also worthwhile and enjoyable leadership-building activities that help to develop stronger leaders. Specific growth areas are the focus of these leadership-building initiatives. Understanding the definition and significance of leadership development areas is essential for developing into a powerful and well-respected leader, whether done through practical exercises or through critical analysis.

The leadership development areas include: Decision making, Communication, Workplace culture, Performance, Mentoring, Accepting change, Building trust, Organization, Creativity and open mindedness, Patience, Adaptation, intuitive, and Emotional Intelligence.

www.ingramcontent.com/pod-product-compliance
Lightning Source LLC
Chambersburg PA
CBHW062333290526
45794CB00005B/2014